Italian Cookbook

50 Italian Recipes
from Breakfast to Dinner

By

Patrick Smith

Copyright © 2015 Patrick Smith

All rights reserved.

ISBN-10: 1511854871
ISBN-13: 978-1511854870

Contents

Section 1: Breakfasts

1. Tomato and Bacon Frittata

A delicious omelet that contains many vitamins and proteins.

8 **Eggs** (lightly beaten)
4 tbs **milk**
¼ cup **parsley** (minced)
2 **green** or **yellow onions** (sliced)
4 **sage** leaves (thinly sliced)
8 **bacon strips** (chopped)
2 **plum tomatoes** (sliced)
2 medium **potatoes** (peeled, thinly sliced)
1 cup **parmesan cheese** (grated)
¼ tsp each **salt** and **pepper**

Makes 8 servings
Calories: 234 per serving

Combine the eggs, milk, parsley, salt and pepper in a large bowl. Mix and set aside.

Place the bacon strips in an ovenproof frying pan and cook until crisp. Remove the bacon from the pan, reserving the drippings.

Add the potatoes, sage and onions to the pan. Cook for 13-15 minutes until browned. If needed, turn potato slices and reduce heat to limit browning. Season with grated cheese.

Pour in the egg mixture and decorate with tomato slices.

Cover the pan, reduce heat to medium-low, and cook for 15 - 20 minutes. Once the eggs are set, remove from heat and transfer to a serving plate. Cut into wedges and serve.

2. Risotto with Italian Sausages

A fast and easy dish that is perfect for breakfast as well as any other time of the day.

4 Italian sausages
1 cup **white rice**
½ cup **white wine**
1 small **onion** (chopped)
3 cups **chicken broth**
2 small **bay leaves**
⅓ cup **Parmesan cheese** (grated)
⅓ cup **Italian parsley** (chopped)
4 tsp **butter** (divided)

Makes 4 servings
Calories: 146 per serving

Melt 2 tbs butter in a large pan over medium heat.

Add sausages, onion and bay leaves. Sauté for about 5 minutes, until the onion is lightly golden and tender.

Add the rice and wine. Bring to a boil and add 3 cups chicken broth. Reduce heat to medium-low and let simmer for about 20 minutes, stirring frequently until rice is tender. If it becomes too dry, add more broth.

Remove bay leaves. Add cheese and parsley. Stir to combine.

Flavor with salt and pepper. Serve and enjoy!

3. Breakfast Strata

A strata is similar to frittata, but voluminous like a cake or lasagna. This one uses milk, eggs and bread.

½ lbs. (225 g) smoked **ham** (cut)
6 **eggs**
3 cups **milk**
2 cups **Gruyere cheese** (grated)
¼ tsp **nutmeg** (grated)
8 cups **French** or **Italian bread**
½ tsp each **salt** and **pepper**

Makes 6 Servings
Calories: 148 per serving

Shred the bread into small pieces. Combine the eggs, milk, salt, pepper, nutmeg and bread pieces in a large bowl. Stir to mix.

Grease a baking dish with butter. Transfer half of the mixture to the baking dish. Spoon half of the cheese over it, then pour in the remaining mixture.

Arrange the ham evenly on top, sprinkling with the remaining cheese. Let the strata stand for at least 25 minutes before baking. If desired, it can also be refrigerated overnight.

Preheat the oven to 350°F (180°C). Bake the strata for about 45 minutes. Once golden and cooked through, withdraw the strata from the oven and let it cool for a few minutes before you serve.

4. Bacon Ricotta Frittata

This frittata is more elaborate and an experience that jump-starts you into the day.

12 large **eggs**
1 cup **shallots** (sliced)
12 oz. (340 g) **bacon** (smoked, cut)
12 oz. (340 g) **assorted greens** (chopped)
1 cup **parmesan cheese** (grated)
12 oz. (340 g) **ricotta cheese**
½ tsp **salt**

Makes 6 servings
Calories: 292 per serving

Preheat the oven to 350°F (180°C). Place bacon in an ovenproof nonstick pan and cook over medium-high heat until crisp.

Transfer bacon to paper towels to drain, reserving 2 tbs of dripping. Transfer the dripping to a bowl for later use.

Add shallots to the pan and fry for 3-4 minutes over medium heat until lightly brown and translucent. Add the greens and continue cooking for about 15 minutes, or until wilted and tender. Transfer greens to a plate and let them cool.

In a large bowl, whisk eggs and salt until mixed well. Stir in ¾ cup parmesan, cooked greens and half of the bacon. Add cheese ricotta last.

In a frying pan, heat 1 tbs reserved dripping over medium heat. Add the egg mixture, spreading the greens evenly. Top with the remaining bacon and ¼ cup parmesan cheese.

Cook over medium heat for about 10 minutes. Once the frittata is set at the edges, transfer to the oven and bake for about 20 minutes.

Remove from the oven and transfer to a serving dish. Let stand for 30 minutes before serving.

5. Asparagus Casserole

This recipe needs to be prepared 1 day before serving, as it includes a 12 hour refrigeration period.
Asparagus is popular in Europe and has many health benefits. This meal combines the flavors of asparagus with red pepper and Swiss cheese (or another melting cheese of your choice).

½ cup **butter**
8 **eggs** (beaten)
1 medium **red pepper** (chopped)
1 medium **onion** (sliced)
8 cups **Italian bread** (cubed)
½ lb. (230 g) **asparagus** (steamed, cut)
2 cups **Swiss cheese** (shredded)
1 cup cooked **ham** (cubed)
2 ½ cups **milk**
½ tsp **marjoram**
½ tsp **salt**
1/8 tsp **pepper**

Makes 12 servings
Calories: 231 per serving

Coat a saucepan with cooking spray. Over medium heat, melt butter in a frying pan. Add steamed asparagus, onion and chopped red pepper. Sauté for about 5 minutes, turning frequently.

Arrange bread, vegetables, ham and 1 cup of grated cheese in the sprayed pan.
Combine milk, eggs and seasonings in a large bowl. Spread evenly over the bread mixture. Cover and refrigerate for at least 12 hours.

Preheat the oven to 350°F (180°C). Bake the mixture for 50 minutes. Once golden, top with the remaining cup of cheese and bake until cheese is melted. Withdraw the casserole from the oven and let cool for 15-20 minutes. Cut in squares and serve.

6. Italian Sausage Muffins

This interesting recipe combines classic Italian ingredients and sausages and turns them into the shape of muffins.

7 oz. (200 g) sweet **Italian sausage**
14 oz. (400 g) **pizza sauce**
⅓ cup **parmesan cheese** (grated)
½ tsp **oregano**
2 tbs **olive oil**
1 **egg**
2 **cups flour**
1 tbs **baking powder**
1/2 tsp **salt**
1/8 tsp **pepper**

Makes 12 servings
Calories: 126 per serving

Preheat the oven to 350°F (180°C)

Place sausages in a skillet and break them up with fork. Sauté without oil until golden brown, then transfer to paper towels to drain. Set aside.

In a large bowl, mix Parmesan cheese, pepper, flour, baking powder and salt.

In another bowl, lightly beat the egg. Add pizza sauce, olive oil, and roasted sausage. Mix well.

Pour the egg mixture over the flour mixture and stir to combine. Grease muffin tins and fill with sausage mix.

Bake in the oven for about 25 minutes until cooked through and golden on top. Remove from the oven and let cool for 30 minutes, before serving.

7. Goat Cheese Frittata and Bell Pepper

This dish is about spices and combines the flavors of cheese with red bell pepper, garlic and basil, producing an unforgettable aftertaste.

½ cup **goat cheese** (crumbled)
1 bunch **scallions** (trimmed, sliced)
2 cloves **garlic** (minced)
10 **eggs**
1 cup **red bell pepper** (sliced)
2 tbs **basil** (finely chopped)
1 tsp **salt**
¼ tsp **black pepper**

Makes 4 servings
Calories: 115 per serving

Preheat broiler.

Combine the eggs, basil, and garlic in a medium bowl. Season with salt and pepper.

Coat a large, ovenproof skillet with cooking spray. Stir in red bell pepper and green onions. Cook for about 1 minute over medium heat, or until the onions are lightly wilted.

Top the vegetables with the egg mixture and cook for 3 minutes. Gently lift the edges of the frittata to make the uncooked egg flow under it.

Once the bottom of the frittata is lightly brown, sprinkle the top with cheese and place the pan in the oven. Grill for 3 minutes. Once lightly golden, remove and let cool 10 minutes before serving.

8. Spinach Gouda Frittata

This combination of spinach, ham and egg whites is delicious and healthy to serve for breakfast.

5 oz. (140 g) baby **spinach** (chopped)
2 cups **egg whites**
¾ cup **Gouda cheese** (shredded)
½ cup **lean ham** (diced)
2 **leeks** (diced)
1/tsp **lemon zest**
1 tsp **garlic powder**
2 tsp **dill** (finely chopped)
½ tsp **salt**
¼ tsp **pepper** (ground)

Makes 6 servings
Calories: 121 per serving

Preheat the oven to 450°F (230°C), placing the rack in upper third position.

In a medium bowl, combine egg whites, garlic powder, salt and pepper.

Coat a large ovenproof skillet with nonfat cooking spray. Pour in fresh dill, leeks and lemon zest. Sauté for about 3-4 minutes, whisking constantly. Add ham and spinach and cook for 1 more minute.

Once spinach is wilted, top vegetables with the egg mixture and cook for 3 minutes.

Gently lift the edges of the frittata to make the uncooked egg flow under it. Flavor the top of the frittata with cheese, place on rack of the preheated oven and bake for 10 minutes.

Remove from the oven and let cool for 5 minutes before serving.

9. Italian Pizza Breakfast

What would Italian cuisine be without pizza? This one works well for breakfast.

5 cups **potatoes**
1 medium **tomato** (thinly sliced)
1 lb. (430 g) **bulk Italian sausage**
1 cup **cheddar cheese** (shredded)
½ cup **mushrooms** (sliced)
½ cup **onion** (chopped)
½ cup **green pepper** (chopped)
4 **eggs**
½ tsp **salt**
Pepper to taste
Sour cream and **salsa** (optional)

Makes 6 Servings
Calories: 210 per serving

In a large frying pan, roast the sausage over medium-high heat until it starts to brown.

Add green pepper, onion, potatoes, and season with salt and pepper. Cook over medium heat for about 20 minutes, or until potatoes are acquiring a golden crust.

Add mushrooms and whisk to combine.

In a small bowl, beat eggs and spoon over potato mixture.

Top the mixture with tomato slices and shredded cheese. Cover on and cook over medium heat for about 12 minutes.

Serve with sour cream and salsa, if desired.

10. Fruity Strata

A strata is similar to frittata, but voluminous like a cake or lasagna. This one features berries, orange flavors and ricotta.

3 tbs **honey**
10 oz. (280 g) frozen mixed **berries**
1 cup whole **milk**
½ cup **ricotta**
2 tbs **butter**
4 large **eggs**
¼ cup **orange juice**
4 slices **bread**
3 tbs **sugar** (optional)

Makes 4 servings
Calories: 326 per serving

Thaw and drain the mixed berries. Tear the bread into small pieces.

Melt the butter in a small saucepan over low heat. Remove from heat, stir in the honey and mix to combine.

Whisk the eggs in a large bowl. Add ricotta, milk, butter, orange juice, bread, berries, honey mixture, and optional sugar.

Transfer the mixture to a 10-inch (25 cm) round baking dish. Cover with plastic wrap and place in the refrigerator for at least 2 hours.

Preheat the oven to 350°F (180°C). Bake the strata for about 40 minutes, or until cooked through and the top is light golden.

Remove from the oven and let cool for 5 minutes before serving.

Section 2: Lunch

1. Eggplants with Ricotta and Spinach

A combination of eggplant and spinach that makes an especially filling meal.

18 oz. (510 g) **spinach**
2 **eggplants** (sliced)
12 oz. (340 g) **tomato-basil sauce**
2 tbs **olive oil**
9 oz. (250 g) **ricotta**
4 tbs **breadcrumbs**
1 ½ oz. (40 g) **onion** (optional)
1 ½ oz. (40 g) **garlic** (optional)
4 tbs **parmesan** or **cheddar cheese**
Nutmeg (grated)
Salt and **pepper**

Makes 5 servings
Calories: 296 per serving

Heat oven to 430°F (220°C).

Peel and slice the eggplants lengthwise. Brush both sides of the slices with the olive oil, place on a baking dish and bake for 17-20 minutes, turning once.

Place the spinach in a colander and pour over a pot of boiling water. Allow to cool, then squeeze out water as much as possible. Combine with the ricotta, some nutmeg, and salt and pepper to taste.

Put a spoonful of the seasoned spinach mix in the center of each eggplant slice, fold it once and place in an ovenproof dish. Spoon over tomato-basil sauce, the optional onion and garlic, then top with breadcrumbs and cheese. Bake for 25 minutes, or until cheese is melted and lightly brown.

2. Parmigiano Risotto

Risotto is a rice meal that can be made in many variations.

1 ½ cups **Arborio rice**
4 medium **yellow onions** (halved, sliced)
1 oz. (30 g) **Parmigiano-Reggiano** cheese (grated)
3 tbs. **olive oil**
2 oz. (60 g) **butter**
4 cups **chicken broth**
½ cup **dry white wine**
Salt and **black pepper**

Makes 5 servings
Calories: 375 per serving

Heat the olive oil in a heavy duty pot over medium-high heat, then add the onions and reduce the heat to medium-low. Cook for about 6 minutes. Season with ¼ tsp salt and continue to cook for about 25 minutes, stirring constantly until the onions are golden.

Combine the broth and 2 cups water in a saucepan. Set over medium heat and bring to a boil.

Transfer the onions to a bowl and cover. Add ½ cup of the broth mixture to the pot, then use a spatula to scrape any stuck bits off the bottom. Transfer to the other broth mixture in the saucepan.

Clean the pot and melt 2 tbs of the butter in it over medium heat. Add the rice and sauté for 1 minute while stirring, until glossy and translucent on the edges. Whisk in the wine and cook for 1 more minute, stirring constantly.

Add enough broth to cover the rice, typically about ½ cup. Let simmer, stirring frequently, until most of the broth has been absorbed. Repeat adding the broth in this way, until the rice is tender but still has some resistance. This should take 25 minutes.

Add the remaining 2 tsp butter, then sprinkle the rice with the grated cheese. Season with salt and pepper to taste. Top with the remaining onions and serve immediately.

3. Kale Pasta with Ricotta and Tomatoes

Fresh basil sauce and cherry tomatoes give this healthy dish a beautiful color – it is also rich in fiber and vitamin C.

18 oz. (500 g) **penne pasta**
7 oz. (200 g) **kale** (chopped)
2 tbs **olive oil**
3 **garlic** cloves (chopped)
1 ¾ lbs. (800 g) **cherry tomatoes**
1 tsp **chili flakes** (crushed)
4 tbs **ricotta**
4 tbs fresh **pesto**
Parmesan (optional)
Salt and **pepper**

Makes 4 servings
Calories: 395 per serving

Cook the pasta according to packaging directions. Add the kale for the final 2 minutes of cooking. Drain the pasta in a colander.

Meanwhile, heat the olive oil in a large saucepan. Add the garlic and sauté for 2 minutes, or until brown. Add the tomatoes and chili flakes, then season with salt and pepper.

Simmer for 15 minutes, or until the sauce thickens. Add the pasta to the sauce and mix to combine.

Transfer the pasta and sauce to four serving bowls. Top each with some ricotta and pesto and drizzle with Parmesan, if desired.

4. Shrimp Tomato Pasta

This recipe combines seafood with tomato and pasta for an extra touch of Mediterranean flavor.

1 lb. (450 g) **large shrimp** (peeled, deveined)
1 lb. (430 g) **linguine pasta** (dried)
2 tbs **olive oil**
1 small **onion** (finely diced)
4 **garlic** cloves (thinly sliced)
6 oz. (170 g) **chorizo** (sliced)
26 oz. (730 g) **tomatoes** (chopped)
¼ tsp **red pepper flakes** (crushed)
¼ cup flat-leaf **parsley** (chopped)
Salt

Makes 5 servings
Calories: 320 per serving

Boil a pot of salted water over high heat and cook the linguine according to packaging instructions. Drain the pasta in a colander.

Meanwhile, heat the olive oil in a large frying pan over medium-high heat. Sauté the sliced chorizo for 3 minutes, turning occasionally.

Add the shrimp and cook for 2 minutes, or until it curls up. Stir occasionally. Transfer the shrimp and chorizo to a bowl. Either reserve 2 tbs of the fat in the pan or add more olive oil. Place the pan over medium heat.

Add the garlic and onion and cook for a few minutes, until tender and lightly golden. Stir in the pepper flakes and the tomatoes with their juices. Simmer for 5 minutes to combine the flavors.

Stir the shrimp and chorizo into the sauce and simmer for another 2 minutes. Season with salt. Transfer the pasta, sauce and parsley to a large serving bowl and serve.

5. Salmon Broccoli Casserole

A delicious casserole with pasta, salmon, anchovy, and broccoli.

9 oz. (250 g) **penne pasta**
10 oz. (280 g) **broccoli** (cut into florets)
8 sundried **tomatoes** (sliced)
4 **salmon fillets** (skinless)
2 oz. (55 g) **cheddar** (grated)
2.5 cups (600 ml) **milk**
1 oz. (30 g) **butter**
8 **anchovy fillets** (halved)
1 oz. (30 g) **flour**
4 oz. (115 g) **mascarpone**
2 tbs **small capers** (rinsed)
10 large **basil leaves** (torn)

Makes 4 servings
Calories: 354 per serving

Preheat the oven to 375°F (190°C).

Place pasta in a large pot of lightly salted boiling water and cook according to packaging instructions.

Add the broccoli and cook for 4 more minutes, or until just softened. Drain in a colander.

In a large pan, combine flour, butter, and milk. Set heat to medium and whisk until it turns into a thick and smooth sauce.

Remove the pan from heat and stir in the mascarpone, capers, anchovies, sun-dried tomatoes, and basil. Add the cooked pasta and broccoli into the mixture and season well to taste.

Halve the salmon fillets and arrange the pieces evenly in an ovenproof dish. Top the fillets with the broccoli mixture and sprinkle with grated cheddar.

Bake in the oven for 30 minutes, or until pale golden. Remove from the oven and let cool for 5 minutes before serving.

6. Parmesan Tomato Quiche

This quiche is full of Italian flavors and is perfect for eating in the garden.

You need a 10 inch (25 cm) tart dish and baking beans for this recipe. Adjust the recipe if you wish to use a different size.

2 oz. (55 g) **parmesan** (grated)
10 oz. (280 g) **cherry tomatoes**
Olive oil
2 **eggs**
1 cup **double cream**
1 handful **basil leaves** (shredded)
10 oz. (280 g) **flour**
5 oz. (140 g) **butter** (cut)
Salt and **pepper**

Makes 7 Servings
Calories: 315 per serving

In a medium bowl, combine the flour and butter until well mixed. Add 9 tbs water, knead with your hands to make dough and roll it into a ball.

Place the dough on a floured surface. With a rolling pin, form the dough into a 12 inch (30 cm) circle. Lift it up and place it over the tart dish so there is an overhang of dough on the sides.

Form a small ball out of pastry scraps and use it to press the dough into the corners of the dish. Refrigerate the dough for 20 minutes before baking.

Preheat the oven to 375°F (190°C).

In a small roasting tin, sprinkle the tomatoes with olive oil and season with salt and pepper. Transfer the tin to a low shelf of the oven.

Gently prick the bottom of the dough all over with a fork. This releases trapped air that would make the bottoms rise up in the oven.

Line the baking dish with a large circle of parchment and arrange baking beans on it. Blind bake the tart for 20 minutes. Remove the beans and parchment, then continue to bake for another 5-10 minutes, or until the top of the tart turns golden.

Remove the tart and tomatoes from the oven.

While baking, beat the eggs in a large bowl. Gradually add the cream, stir in the basil and season to taste.
When the tart is ready, sprinkle half the cheese over the base, then add with tomatoes and cream mix. Coat the top of the tart with the remaining cheese.

Bake in the oven for 20-25 minutes, or until cooked through and golden brown.

Withdraw from the oven and let it cool for a while. Garnish with the remaining basil. Slice and serve.

7. Chicken Mozzarella Pizza

A pizza topped with chicken breast, red pepper and cheese.

1 tbs **butter**
4 oz. (115 g) **mozzarella cheese** (shredded)
4 oz. (115 g) boneless **chicken breast** (cut)
1/2 **onion** (thinly sliced)
2 tbs **pesto**
1 ⅓ cups **flour**
1 tsp **dry yeast**
½ tbs **sugar** (optional)
½ tbs **olive oil**
1 tsp **salt**
1 sweet **red pepper** (chopped)

Makes 4 servings
Calories: 218 per serving

In a large bowl, dissolve the yeast with ½ cup warm water. Add the olive oil, ½ cup flour, ½ tsp salt, and optional sugar into the mixture. Add the remaining flour and beat the mixture until it turns into a homogeneous mixture.

Place the mixture on a lightly floured surface. Knead the dough until it becomes smooth and elastic. Transfer to floured bowl, cover and set aside in a warm place. Let the dough rise until it has doubled in volume.

Season the chicken with salt, place in a skillet with melted butter and cook over medium heat for about 10-15 minutes. Once it starts to brown, remove the chicken from heat and set aside.

Heat the oven to 425°F (220°C).

On a floured surface, roll the dough into a circle. Transfer the dough to a pizza pan. Spread pesto on the dough and top with onion, chicken, and red pepper. Sprinkle with cheese.

Bake the pizza until crust and cheese is melted and lightly golden.

8. Fettuccine Pasta with Arugula

A delicious pasta dish with Italian sausage and red peppers.

8 oz. (220 g) **Italian sausage** (cut)
10 oz. (730 g) **fettuccine pasta**
13 oz. (830 g) roasted **red peppers** (chopped)
4 cups **baby arugula**
2 tbs. **olive oil**
2 **cloves garlic** (minced)
½ cup **heavy cream**
¾ oz. (20 g) **Parmigiano-Reggiano** (freshly grated)
8 **basil leaves** (thinly sliced)
Salt and **black pepper**

Makes 4 servings
Calories: 236 per serving

Place a large saucepan of salted water over high heat and bring to boil. Cook the pasta in the boiling water following the package directions.

At the same time, heat the olive oil in a skillet over medium heat. Cut the sausage and transfer the pieces to the skillet. Sauté for 5 minutes, stirring frequently.

Once the sausage is cooked through and lightly browned, remove it from the skillet and set aside. Reserve about 1 tbs of the drippings in the skillet. Add the garlic and cook for 30 seconds. Stir in the peppers and cream, reduce the heat to low and simmer for about 7 minutes, or until the sauce is thickened.

The pasta should be finished now. Drain it in a colander and transfer to a large serving bowl. Add the sauce, arugula, cheese, and basil and toss to combine. Season with salt and pepper to taste and serve.

9. Tomato and Cheese Tart

This tart is an ideal way to enjoy seasonal tomatoes and mixed herbs.

4 medium **tomatoes** (sliced)
10 oz. (280 g) **flour**
5 oz. (140 g) **butter** (cut)
2 oz. **Gruyere** (grated)
⅓ cup **mayonnaise**
1 tsp. fresh **oregano** or **marjoram** (finely chopped)
¼ cup mixed **herbs** (chopped)
Salt and **black pepper**

Makes 5 servings
Calories: 215 per serving

Preheat the oven to 425°F (220°C).

In a medium bowl, combine the flour and butter until well mixed. Add 9 tbs water and knead it to make dough, then roll it into a ball.

Place the dough on a floured surface. With a rolling pin, form the dough into a 13 inch (33 cm) circle. Lightly dust it with flour to keep it from sticking.

Transfer the dough to a large rimmed baking sheet. Place the tomatoes evenly on the dough. Lightly season with salt.

Combine mayonnaise, mixed herbs, pepper and cheese in a small bowl. Spoon the mixture over the tomatoes.

Bake for about 25 minutes in the preheated oven, or until the edges acquire a golden-brown crust and the tomatoes are softened.

Remove from the oven and let it cool for about 30 minutes. Cut into wedges and serve.

10. Easy Lasagna

A fast and easy lasagna, featuring three types of cheese.

25 oz. (700 g) **spaghetti sauce**
9 **lasagna noodles**
8 oz. (225 g) **cottage cheese**
3 cups **mozzarella cheese** (grated)
¾ cup **parmesan cheese**
1 **egg**

Makes 8 servings
Calories: 325 per serving

Pour some of the sauce into 13 x 9 inch (33 x 23 cm) pan.

Place 3 lasagna noodles on the sauce.

In a bowl combine egg, cottage cheese and parmesan cheese.

Spread ⅓ of the egg-cheese mixture over noodles. Add ⅓ of the sauce. Top the noodles with 1 cup mozzarella. Add 3 more noodles. Repeat this paragraph two more times. You should end up with mozzarella on top.

Transfer the pan to the oven and bake in 350°F (180°C) for about 1 hour, or until the top of lasagna is golden and bubbly.

Serve and enjoy!

Section 3: Side Dishes

1. Vegetable Risotto

A tasty risotto made with vegetable broth, cream, mushrooms and a variety of fresh vegetables. It can be served either as a side dish or main course.

1 cup **rice**
1 cup whole **milk**
1 cup **Parmesan cheese** (grated)
1 ½ cups **mushrooms** (sliced)
5 cups **vegetable stock**
3 small **onions** (chopped)
1 clove **garlic** (crushed)
1 tsp **parsley** (minced)
1 tsp **celery** (minced)
1 tbs **olive oil**
¼ cup **heavy cream**
1 tsp **butter**
Salt and **pepper** to taste

Makes 4 servings
Calories: 267 per serving

Heat olive oil in a large pan over medium-high heat. Cook the onion and garlic in the olive oil until the onion translucent and the garlic is lightly golden. Discard the garlic. Stir in celery and parsley, then season with salt and pepper.

Cook until celery is softened. Add the mushrooms and reduce heat to low. Let simmer until the mushrooms are tender.

Pour the milk, cream, and vegetable stock into the skillet. Add the rice and let simmer until all liquid is absorbed.

Once the rice is cooked, add the butter and sprinkle with Parmesan cheese. Remove the pan from heat. Serve hot.

2. Italian Pasta Salad

A delicious salad with fresh bell peppers and two types of dressing.

1 red **bell pepper** (diced)
1 green **bell pepper** (chopped)
16 oz. (450 g) **rotini pasta**
1 red **onion,** (diced)
1 cup **Parmesan cheese** (grated)
1 cup **Italian dressing**
1 cup **Caesar dressing**

Makes 11 servings
Calories: 244 per serving

Cook pasta according to packaging instructions. Rinse under cold water and drain in a colander. Transfer to a large bowl, then add the bell peppers, red onion, Italian dressing and Caesar dressing.

Mix until well combined. Sprinkle the salad with grated parmesan cheese.

Serve either chilled or at room temperature.

3. Fried Eggplant

A fast and easy eggplant dish that combines parmesan and garlic flavors.

Olive oil (for the skillet)
1 **eggplant** (sliced)
Fresh **breadcrumbs**
½ cup **flour**
½ tbs **garlic powder** (optional)
1 tbs **parmesan cheese**
2 **eggs**
½ tsp **salt**

Makes 6 servings
Calories: 95 per serving

In a small bowl, beat eggs and season with salt and optional garlic powder. Combine cheese with breadcrumbs.

Coat eggplant slices with cornstarch. Shake off excess, then dunk into beaten egg.

Coat the slices with the breadcrumb-cheese mix and roast them in a skillet until it acquires a golden crust. Season with salt to taste.

4. Tomato Bread Salad

This is an ideal side dish for a garden party.

12 **olives** (pitted, halved)
4 **tomatoes** (chopped)
8 oz. (220 g) **sourdough bread** (toasted)
4 oz. (110 g) low fat **mozzarella** (cubed)
½ red **onion** (diced)
¼ cup **basil** (shredded)
1 **garlic clove** (minced)
2 tbs **olive oil** (optional)
2 tbs **red wine vinegar**
2 tbs **balsamic vinegar**
1 tsp **salt**
½ tsp **pepper**

Makes 4 servings
Calories: 249 per serving

In a small bowl, soak diced red onion in water to dilute its taste and make it milder.

Preheat the oven to 400°F (200°C). Place sliced bread on a baking sheet and toast it in the oven for about 10 minutes.

Remove it from the oven and let it cool. At the same time, combine all ingredients except for the onion and bread in a large bowl and mix well.

Break up the toasted bread into small pieces, drain onions and add to tomato mixture. Toss to combine. Season with salt and pepper, then serve.

5. Chicken Salad in Pasta Shells

A delicious treat for you and all your guests!

1 cup **chicken** (cooked, chopped)
1 lb. (450 g) jumbo **pasta shells**
¾ cup **cucumber** (coarsely chopped)
4 cups **romaine lettuce** (chopped)
1 cup **tomato** (coarsely chopped)
3 oz. (85 g) **hard salami** (chopped)
½ cup **basil** (chopped)
⅓ cup **garlic vinaigrette dressing** (roasted)

Makes 10 servings
Calories: 154 per serving

Cook pasta shells according to packaging directions. Drain in a colander and set aside to cool.

In a medium bowl, combine the chicken, lettuce, salami, cucumber, basil and tomato. Spoon vinaigrette over the salad, then toss to mix.

Fill the shells with the salad. Cover and place in the fridge for 2 hours before serving.

6. Cheesy Tomatoes

An easy side dish for any meal. The addition of chopped onions gives it a nice crunch and blends the flavors well together.

4 oz. (120 g) **butter** (melted)
½ cup **breadcrumbs**
4 **tomatoes** (cut in half, seeded)
½ cup **parmesan cheese**
1 small **onion** (finely chopped)
3 tbs **parsley**, (chopped)
2 tbs **chives,** (chopped)
1 tsp **tarragon**
1 tsp **pepper**

Makes 8 servings
Calories: 152 per serving

Combine bread crumbs, parmesan cheese, chives, parsley and tarragon in a medium bowl. Season with pepper. Add onion and melted butter. Mix to combine.

Preheat the oven 350°F (180°C). Grease the baking dish with butter.

Fill the seeded tomato halves with the breadcrumbs mixture. Transfer to a baking dish and bake in the oven for about 10 minutes. Remove from the oven and let cool for at least 5 minutes before serving.

7. Vegetable Prosciutto

Prosciutto works well with any vegetable. This side dish combines it with broccoli and onion.

4 slices **Italian prosciutto** (cut into strips)
¼ cup **olive oil**
1 medium **onion** (chopped)
1 ½ lbs. (680 g) **broccoli** (cut into florets)
1 **garlic clove** (chopped)
Salt

Makes 4 servings
Calories: 157 per serving

Set a large pot of salted water over high heat and bring to a boil. Add broccoli florets and cook for about 5 minutes, or until broccoli is partially tender.

Remove and rinse under cold water. Combine oil, onion and garlic in the same pot and sauté over medium heat for 10 minutes, or until brown. Stir in broccoli, then cover and reduce heat to low. Simmer for 15 minutes.

Break up the broccoli with a fork. Add prosciutto to the dish and toss to coat. Season with salt and pepper. Serve hot.

8. Classic Peperonata

Peperonata is a classic Italian dish that combines tomatoes, onions and bell peppers.

1 large **onion**, (sliced)
4 **garlic** cloves (thinly sliced)
2 **red bell peppers** (sliced)
2 **green bell peppers** (sliced)
2 **yellow bell peppers** (sliced)
¼ cup **olive oil**
1 tbs **oregano** (dried)
½ cup **basil**
5 **plum tomatoes** (seeded, diced)
Salt and **pepper** to taste

Makes 5 servings
Calories: 106 per serving

Heat olive oil in a large skillet on medium-high heat. Add the onions, season with salt and cook for about 3 minutes, or until the onions are just golden.

Stir in the peppers and fry for another 5 minutes, stirring frequently. Once the peppers are tender, add the garlic and sauté for 2 minutes.

Sprinkle with a little more salt and add the oregano. Cook 1 more minute and stir in the tomato dices. Remove from heat and add the basil.

Season with pepper before serving.

9. Roasted Stuffing

A stuffing recipe that combines many Mediterranean flavors. It takes a while to prepare but is well worth it.

14 oz. (400 g) **tomatoes** (stewed)
10 oz. (300 g) **Italian sausage**
¾ lb. (340 g) **mushrooms** (finely sliced)
3 **eggs**
1 **white onion** (finely chopped)
4 **garlic cloves** (sliced)
1/8 tsp **red pepper flakes**
1 tbs **basil** (chopped)
2 tbs **olive oil**
¾ cup **white wine**
¾ cups **Romano cheese** (grated)
1 ½ cups **Italian Bread Crumbs**
1 tbs **parsley** (chopped)
1 **bay leaf**

Makes 5 servings
Calories: 284 per serving

Preheat the oven to 350°F (180°C).

Heat olive oil in a skillet over medium heat. Add the sausage and sauté for 4 minutes. Remove and set aside.

Remove all but 3 tbs of the drippings left in the skillet. Stir in the onions, red pepper flakes, garlic, mushrooms and bay leaf. Sauté for 10 minutes, stirring frequently. Add the wine and cook for 5 minutes, or until it has evaporated.

Drain the stewed tomatoes in a colander, reserving their juice in a cup. Roughly chop the tomatoes and add them to the skillet, along with basil, parsley, and the reserved juice. Stir to mix, then cook over medium-low heat for 5 minutes, stirring occasionally, until the mixture is thickened. Pour the mixture to a large bowl.

Beat the eggs in a bowl until smooth, then pour them over the tomato mixture. Add 1 cup of the bread crumbs and grated cheese.

Grease a baking dish with butter, sprinkle with the remaining bread crumbs. Fill the tomato-egg mixture into the dish and bake in the oven for about 25 minutes. Remove from the oven and serve.

10. Cauliflower Gratin

This is a traditional Italian dish. It features a plethora of flavors and is a bit more demanding to make, but well worth the effort.

4 **garlic cloves**, (thickly sliced)
1 ½ tsp **rosemary** (chopped)
¼ tsp **red pepper flakes**
1 tbs **anchovy paste**
1 tbs **capers** (drained)
4 tbs **olive oil**
4 tsp **Italian parsley** (chopped)
1 lb. (450 g) **cauliflower florets** (cut)
3 tbs **Italian Bread Crumbs**
3 tbs **Pecorino Romano cheese** (grated)
1/8 tsp black **pepper**

Makes 4 servings
Calories: 240 per serving

Preheat your broiler.

Heat the olive oil in a saucepan over medium-high heat. Add the garlic, red pepper flakes, anchovy paste, capers, rosemary, and 3 tsp of the parsley. Season with black pepper and sauté for 3 minutes, or until the garlic is golden.

Add the cauliflower and toss to coat. Cook for 2 minutes, or until the cauliflower turns brown on all sides. Remove the cauliflower from the pan and add it into to a small baking dish.

In a small bowl, combine the grated cheese and bread crumbs. Top the cauliflower with this mixture. Place in the broiler for 5 minutes, or until the bread crumbs and cheese are golden and fragrant.

Garnish with the remaining parsley and serve.

Section 4: Snacks

1. Tomato Bruschetta

This crispy bruschetta can be served as a starter or delicious snack with a glass of cold white wine.

2 tbs **olive oil**
2 cup **tomatoes** (chopped)
1 small **onion**
3 **garlic** cloves
5 **basil** leaves
16 slices **Italian bread**
Salt and **black pepper**

Makes 4 servings
Calories: 95 per serving

Place chopped tomatoes in a medium bowl. Add thinly sliced onions, garlic and basil leaves. Season the vegetables with salt and pepper to taste. Drizzle with olive oil.

Toast the bread slices. Arrange the tomato mixture on the slices and serve.

2. Pork Sandwiches

These Italian sandwiches combine garlic and rosemary with provolone cheese. Each flavor contributes to a sensation that is greater than the sum of its parts.

2 ¾ lbs. (1.25 kg) boneless **pork loin**
½ tsp **red pepper** (dried, crushed)
2 tbs **garlic** (minced)
12 oz. (340 g) **provolone cheese** (slices smoked)
6 **hoagie rolls** (split)
1 bunch **broccoli**
1 ½ tbs **rosemary** (finely chopped)
7 tbs **olive oil** (divided)
1 tbs **salt**
2 tsp **black pepper**

Makes 6 servings
Calories: 105 per serving

Combine the garlic, rosemary, and 3 tbs olive oil in a small bowl. Season with salt and pepper.

Place pork on a baking dish. Spoon the garlic mixture over the pork and gently rub it in. Cover and refrigerate for at least 2 hours.

Before removing the pork from the fridge, turn preheat the grill to 400°C (200°C).

Place the baking dish in the oven and grill for 30 minutes, or until cooked through. Remove from grill, and let cool 5 minutes before slicing.

Cut broccoli into florets and cook them in a medium pot of boiling water for about 6 minutes. Drain and rinse under cold water, reserving ½ cup cooking water.

Heat remaining 4 tbs olive oil in a large pan over medium heat. Add remaining garlic, red pepper, and broccoli. Sauté for 5 minutes. Add reserved ½ cup water and continue cooking for another 2 minutes.

Place a cheese slice on the bottom half of each hoagie roll. Add pork and broccoli on the top of cheese. Cover with the tops of the rolls and serve.

3. Potato Wedges

An easy but delicious potato recipe that is especially popular with kids.

3 potatoes
2 ½ tbs **olive oil**
½ tbs **basil** (dried)
½ tbs **oregano** (dried)
2 ½ tbs **parmesan cheese** (grated)
½ tsp **garlic salt**

Makes 4 servings
Calories: 99 per serving

Preheat the oven to 425°F (220°C)

Halve potatoes lengthwise, then quarter each half to make wedges. Place the wedges on a baking sheet with the skin side down.

In a small bowl, combine the oil, garlic powder and herbs.

Spread the oil mixture evenly on each potato wedge. Top the wedges with the grated cheese.

Bake in the oven for about 30 minutes. Remove and let cool for 5 minutes before serving.

4. Crispy Salmon Sticks

Italian seafood, featuring fish sticks made from salmon fillet.

3 **egg whites**
1 cup **Parmesan** (grated)
17 oz. (480 g) **salmon fillet** (skinned)
½ cup **flour**
1 tbs **Dijon mustard**
1 cup **bread crumbs** (seasoned)
1 tbs **parsley** or **chives** (chopped)
⅓ cup **mayonnaise**
⅓ cup **plain yogurt**
Olive oil
½ tsp s**ea salt**
¼ tsp **black pepper**

Makes 5 servings
Calories: 210 per serving

In a small dipping bowl, combine the mayonnaise, yogurt, Dijon mustard, and parsley (or chives). Stir to mix.

Preheat the oven to 450°F (230°C). Rinse the salmon fillet and dry thoroughly with paper towels. Slice in equal square pieces.

In a medium bowl and combine flour, salt and pepper. Beat the egg whites in another bowl. Combine the Parmesan and bread crumbs in a third bowl.

Coat the salmon pieces in the flour mix. Dunk the floured salmon into the egg whites, then into the Parmesan mixture.

Arrange the breaded salmon pieces on an oiled baking dish. Drizzle lightly with olive oil. Cook in the oven for about 20 minutes, or until crispy and golden brown.

Transfer the fish sticks on a serving dish. Serve with the mayonnaise-yogurt sauce for dipping.

5. Apple Cinnamon Muffins

This recipe is a real treat, combining the flavor of cinnamon, sugar and apples.

1 ½ cups **apples** (peeled, chopped)
½ tsp **cinnamon** (ground)
2 ⅔ cup **flour**
½ cup **olive oil**
1 ½ tsp **baking powder**
1 ½ tsp **baking soda**
¾ cup **yogurt**
2 **eggs**
⅔ cup **sugar**
½ tsp **salt**

Topping:
4 tbs **flour**
3 tbs **oats**
¼ cup **sugar**
½ tsp **cinnamon** (ground)
2 tbs **olive oil**

Makes 12 servings
Calories: 254 per serving

Preheat the oven to 350°F (180°C). Coat a muffin tin with non-stick spray or line with papers.

In a large bowl, combine flour, baking soda, baking powder, cinnamon, and salt.
In another bowl, beat together the eggs, sugar, oil, and yogurt until smooth. Combine the wet and dry ingredients. Stir until blended.

Add the apple pieces and stir. Spoon the batter into 12 muffin cups. Place the topping ingredients in a small bowl and mix.

Sprinkle a little of the topping mix over each muffin, then bake for about 20 minutes.

Remove from the oven and let cool for 5 minutes before serving.

6. Cheesy Spinach Calzone

Crispy pizza pockets that are filled with cheese and spinach.

⅓ cup **pancetta** or **bacon** (diced, cooked until crisp)
5 oz. (150 g) **spinach** (frozen, chopped)
6 oz. (170 g) **pizza dough**
1 dash of **red pepper flakes**
1 cup **ricotta cheese**
1 **egg**
All-purpose flour
¼ cup + 4 tbs **parmesan cheese** (grated)
½ cup **mozzarella cheese** (grated)
Salt and **black pepper** to taste

Makes 2 servings
Calories: 341 per serving

Preheat oven to 450°F (230°C).

Coat a baking dish with flour. Roll the dough into 2 balls on a lightly floured surface.

In a bowl, combine the spinach, ricotta, mozzarella, ¼ cup parmesan, and red pepper flakes. Season with salt and pepper to taste.

Spoon half of the filling onto one half the dough circles leaving a small border around the edge. Repeat with the other dough circle.

Fold the other half of the dough over the filling, pushing in the edges to seal.
Put each calzone on the prepared baking dish.

In a small bowl, whisk the egg with a tablespoon of water and beat with a fork until mixed well. Brush each of the calzone with the egg mixture and top with 4 tbs parmesan cheese.

Bake the calzone for 20 to 25 minutes, or until golden brown and crispy. Remove from the oven and let cool for 5 minutes before serving.

7. Vegetable Mozzarella Salad Stack

This recipe combines fresh tomatoes and cucumbers with the flavor of mozzarella.

1 tbs **olive oil**
¼ red **onion** (thinly sliced)
3 **garlic** cloves (minced)
Mozzarella cheese (sliced)
1 medium **cucumber** (sliced)
3 **tomatoes** (sliced)
7 large **basil leaves** (chopped)
3 tbs **balsamic vinegar**
1 pinch **red pepper flakes**

Makes 6 servings
Calories: 73 per serving

In a bowl, combine vinegar with oil, then gradually pour in sugar and red pepper flakes. Mix until the flakes are well drained.

Arrange on a serving plate in this order: cucumber, onion, tomato and mozzarella. Top with the sauce and let stand for 1-2 hours for the vinaigrette to marinate.

Serve and enjoy!

8. Mushroom Fontina Pizza

This pizza is a real party for mushroom lovers. Very nice change from the standard tomato and meat pizza.

Pizza dough
3 cups **mushrooms** (sliced)
4 cups **onions** (thinly sliced)
3 **garlic** cloves (minced)
3 tbs **olive oil**
8 oz. (225 g) **Fontina cheese** (sliced)
Parsley (chopped)
2 tsp **rosemary** (chopped)
Salt and **pepper** to taste

Makes 12 servings
Calories: 115 per serving

Preheat oven to 375°F (190°C)

Lay pizza dough on a baking tray or a round pizza sheet. Top with cheese slices.

In a large skillet, heat 2 tbs olive oil over medium-low heat. Add onions, cover and sauté for 12 minutes, stirring occasionally. Once the onions are tender, remove cover and cook over medium heat for another 8 minutes, or until onions are brown. Transfer to a bowl and set aside.

In the same skillet, place mushrooms, remaining 1 tbs olive oil, garlic, and rosemary. Sauté over medium heat until mushrooms are tender and lightly brown. Pour mushroom mixture over cheese. Spoon the onions on top of the pizza.

Bake in the preheated oven for 25-30 minutes, or until the edges of pizza are slightly crisp and brown. Remove from the oven, season with salt and pepper to taste and let stand for 5 minutes.

Garnish with parsley. Cut the pizza into square pieces and serve immediately.

9. Cheesy Garlic Bread

A crunchy Italian bread, imbued with cheese and garlic flavor.

1 cup **parmesan cheese** (grated)
1 loaf **Italian bread** (thickly sliced)
¾ cup **mayonnaise**
Olive oil
6 **garlic** cloves (minced)
½ tsp **parsley flakes** (dried)
¼ tsp **salt** (optional)

Makes 6 servings
Calories: 272 per serving

Brush one side of the bread slices with olive oil. Lightly toast the bread under the broiler, until it begins to brown.

In a small bowl, combine the parmesan, garlic, mayonnaise, and salt. Spread the garlic mixture over the bread.

Set the bread back under the broiler until the tops are just brown.

Decorate with parsley flakes and serve.

10. Dinner Roll Antipasto

Antipasto means appetizer. This one uses crescent roll dough and combines them with cheeses, ham, and garlic.

16 oz. (450 g) **crescent roll dough** (bought)
Butter
12 oz. (340 g) **bell peppers** (roasted)
4 oz. (115 g) **salami** (sliced)
4 oz. (115 g) **Swiss cheese** (sliced)
4 oz. (115 g) **cheddar cheese**
4 oz. (115 g) **ham** (cooked, sliced)
4 oz. (115 g) **provolone cheese** (sliced)
½ tsp **garlic powder**
2 ¼ oz. (70 g) **olives** (drained, sliced)
2 **eggs** + 1 **egg yolk** (beaten)
½ tsp **pepper**

Makes 6 Servings
Calories: 251 per serving

Preheat oven to 350°F (180°C). Grease a 13 x 9 inch (33 x 23 cm) pan with butter and spray with cooking spray.

Roll out half of the dough into a rectangle and place in the pan. Arrange all meats and cheese on the dough in this order: salami, cheddar cheese, Swiss cheese, ham, provolone cheese.

In a small bowl, whisk in 2 eggs, ground pepper and garlic powder. Pour the mixture over the layers on the dough, then top with roasted bell peppers and olives.

Roll out the second can of dough into a large rectangle and top over the layered ingredients. Push edges to seal.

Brush the top dough with beaten egg yolk, cover with foil and bake for 30 minutes. Remove foil and bake for another 15 minutes, or until the top is golden brown.

Remove from the oven, cut into squares and serve.

Section 5: Dinner

1. Pancetta Meatloaf

A delicious meatloaf made from Italian pancetta ham.

17 oz. (480 g) **lean beef** (minced)
3 ½ oz. (100 g) **pancetta ham** (chopped)
2 oz. (55 g) white **breadcrumbs**
1 **egg** (beaten)
4 tbs **parmesan cheese** (grated)
1 **onion** (finely chopped)
1 **garlic clove** (chopped)
1 tsp **tomato purée**

Makes 4 servings
Calories: 265 per serving

Preheat the oven to 375°F (190°C). Line a baking dish with baking paper.

In a small bowl, combine 2 tbs of breadcrumbs and 2 tbs of Parmesan.

In a large bowl, combine beef, pancetta, egg, onion, garlic clove and 1 tbs tomato puree. Season with salt and pepper and mix.

Press the mixture into the baking dish and season with the crumb mix. Bake in the oven for about 45 minutes, or until the top is golden-brown and crispy.

Remove from the oven and let cool for 5 minutes. Transfer to a serving plate and slice the loaf. Serve with green beans and potatoes.

2. Chicken with Cacciatore Sauce

This is a must-try for poultry lovers. It will take you a while to prepare, but the experience is well worth it.

3 slices **bacon** (chopped)
¼ medium **onion**
8 **chicken thighs**
4 oz. (115 g) **mushrooms**
¼ cup **dry red wine**
1 tbs **olive oil**
⅓ cup **olives** (pitted)
1 tsp fresh **rosemary** leaves
28 oz. (580 g) **tomatoes**
Salt and **pepper**

Makes 4 servings
Calories: 341 per serving

Preheat to 475°F (250°C), setting a rack in the upper third of the oven.

Season the chicken thighs with salt and pepper. Place in a shallow baking pan and bake for about 35 minutes, or until the chicken is golden brown and cooked through.

Meanwhile, place the bacon, onion, mushrooms and rosemary in a blender and pulse until chopped well. Heat olive oil in a large skillet over medium-high heat. Add the vegetable, season with ¼ tsp salt, cover and cook for 7-8 minutes, stirring frequently.

Puree the tomatoes in the blender. Add the wine to the skillet and bring to a boil. Cook for about 3 minutes, or until the wine has almost evaporated.

Add the pureed tomatoes and let boil. Reduce the heat to low and let simmer for about 20 minutes, stirring frequently, until slightly thickened. Sprinkle with salt and pepper. Serve the chicken with the sauce.

3. Italian Roasted Sausage with Veggies

This is a quick and easy recipe that offers a great mix of ingredients. It is an ideal breakfast for a Sunday morning.

8 oz. (230 g) **Italian sausage**
1 ½ lbs. (700 g) small **potatoes** (diced)
3 tbs **olive oil**
1 small **onion**, (sliced)
3 tbs **butter**
1 small **red bell pepper** (diced)
1 small **yellow pepper** (diced)
1 tbs **rosemary** (finely chopped)
2 tbs flat-leaf **parsley** (finely chopped)
3 cloves **garlic** (pasted)
1 tsp **paprika**
3 tbs **olive oil**
Salt and **black pepper**

Makes 4 servings
Calories: 254 per serving

Melt the butter in a large shallow roasting pan over medium-high heat. Add the onions and garlic and sauté for 2 to 3 minutes, or until light golden and tender. Add the peppers and cook another 2 minutes.

Stir in the sausage, potatoes, and paprika. Season with salt and pepper. Cook for about 2 minutes, stirring frequently.

Add the rosemary and begin pressing the mixture against the pan, in order for the bottom to acquire a golden crust and the potatoes to stick together. Whisk the mixture occasionally to divide the crispy bits.

Sprinkle the mixture with parsley. Transfer to a dish, drizzle with olive oil and serve.

4. Roasted Tilapia

Tilapia combined with parsley, pepper and lemon.

3 large **eggs**
1 ½ cups **milk**
4 tbs **butter**
4 each 6 oz. (120 g) **tilapia fillets**
1 cup **flour**
⅓ cup **parsley leaves**
6 cups **baby arugula**
6 slices **white bread** (torn into pieces)
½ **lemon** zest (finely grated) and **lemon wedges**
6 tbs **olive oil**
Salt and **pepper**

Makes 4 servings
Calories: 384 per serving

Preheat the oven to 425°F (220°C).

In a bowl, combine the fish and milk. Let stand for 15 minutes. In a shallow dish, combine the flour, ½ tsp salt, and ½ tsp pepper.

In a bowl, lightly beat the eggs until smooth. Place the parsley bread, lemon zest and ½ tsp salt in a blender. Blend until small crumbs form. Remove from the blender and transfer to a plate.

Remove the fillets from the milk and coat with the flour. Pat to remove excess flour. Dip the fillets in the eggs, then coat all sides with the breadcrumbs. Transfer to a large plate.

Line a baking dish with foil. Heat 2 tbs butter and olive oil in a large frying pan over medium-high heat. Add fillets to the pan and roast for about 3 minutes on each side, or until they begin to brown. Transfer fillets to the baking dish, place in the oven and bake for about 10 minutes.

Drizzle the arugula with remaining olive oil, season with salt and pepper to taste. Garnish the fish with lemon wedges and serve.

5. Ravioli with Veggies

This is an easy recipe to prepare and a perfect dish for gatherings.

¼ cup butter (melted)
¼ cup Parmesan cheese (shredded)
1 lb. (450 g) vegetables (frozen)
1 ½ lbs. (700 g) cheese ravioli (frozen)
¼ tsp seasoning blend

Makes 6 servings
Calories: 324 per serving

Place the vegetables in a large saucepan with boiling water and let cook for 5 minutes. Add ravioli, cook for another 5 minutes, until vegetables are softened. Remove the water.

Add the butter and flavor with seasoning. Top the dish with cheese and serve.

6. Filled Pastry Shell

A delicious pastry shell filled with ingredients.

1 lb. (450 g) **Italian Sausage**
1 egg
1 ½ cups **potatoes** (mashed)
1 unbaked **pastry shell**
8 oz. (230 g) **cottage cheese**
1/4 cup **sour cream**
1 cup (220 g) **cheddar cheese** (shredded)
Cherry tomatoes (quartered)
Parsley (minced)
½ tsp **oregano** (dried)
½ to ¾ tsp **salt**
1/8 tsp **pepper**
2 tsp **butter** (melted)

Makes 6 servings
Calories: 285 per serving

Preheat the oven to 450°F (230°C).

Line the pastry shell with foil and bake in the oven for 7 minutes. Remove from the oven and remove foil. Set aside. Reduce heat to 350°F (180°C)

In a medium pan, cook sausage until beginning to brown. Transfer to paper towels to drain.

Place cottage cheese and egg in a blender and pulse until smooth. Transfer to a large bowl. Add potatoes, oregano, and sour cream to the cheese mixture. Season with salt and pepper, mix to combine.

Place sausage in the pastry shell and spoon the potato mixture over it. Sprinkle with butter. Bake for 50-60 minutes. Top the pastry shell with cheese and let stand until melted. Decorate with tomatoes and parsley.

7. Spaghetti with Meatballs

No archive of Italian recipes would be complete with an elaborate spaghetti dish.

16 oz. (450 g) **spaghetti**

Sauce:
½ cup **onion** (chopped)
2 cloves **garlic** (smashed, minced)
Parmesan cheese
3 tbs **olive oil**
1 tsp **oregano**
½ tsp **basil**
2 lbs. (900 g) **tomatoes** (crushed)
2 tsp **salt** and ¼ tsp **black pepper**

Meatballs:
2 lbs. (900 g) **lean beef** (ground)
½ cup **onion** (finely chopped)
2 **eggs**
1 clove **garlic** (minced)
½ cup **milk**
3 slices **bread** (crumbled)
2 tbs **parsley** (chopped)
1 tsp **salt** and ½ tsp **pepper**

Makes 6 servings
Calories: 254 per serving

Preheat oven to 450°F (230°C).

Start with making the meatballs. Whisk eggs in a large bowl, add bread and milk. Let stand for 3 minutes. Add onion, garlic, parsley, beef, salt and pepper, and mix until all ingredients are well combined. Shape into equal meatballs.

Coat a baking dish with olive oil, arrange the meatballs on it and bake in the oven for 25 minutes.

For the sauce, heat oil in a skillet over medium heat. Add onion and sauté until light golden. Stir in garlic, oregano, basil, and tomatoes. Season with salt and pepper to taste. Once boiling, reduce heat to low. Simmer for about 25 minutes.

Add toasted meatballs to the mixture and cover to keep warm as you cook the spaghetti. Cook spaghetti following to package directions and drain well. Transfer spaghetti to a serving dish, top with meatballs, sprinkle with grated parmesan and serve.

8. Chicken Macaroni Soup

A delicious chicken pasta soup filled with Italian flavors.

1 medium onion (chopped)
1 garlic clove (minced)
1 lb. (450 g) boneless chicken breasts (cubed)
1 ¾ lbs. (800 g) tomatoes (crushed)
14 oz. (400 g) chicken stock
1 medium green bell pepper (chopped)
1 medium red bell pepper (chopped)
½ tsp red pepper flakes (crushed)
1 small carrot (thinly sliced)
1 celery rib (thinly sliced)
3 tbs Parmesan cheese (grated)
1 tsp Italian seasoning
1 cup elbow macaroni (uncooked)
7 tbs mozzarella cheese (shredded)
¼ tsp salt
¼ tsp pepper

Makes 7 servings
Calories: 196 per serving

Coat a nonstick slow cooker with cooking spray. Place the chicken in it and cook over medium heat until pale. Transfer to a bowl and cover to keep warm.

Place carrot, bell peppers, celery and onion in a pan and cook over medium heat, stirring occasionally, until vegetables are softened.

Add the garlic and cook for 1 minute. Pour in water and add the cooked chicken, tomatoes, chicken stock, Parmesan cheese, and seasonings. Bring to a boil, then reduce heat and let simmer for about 40 minutes.

Add macaroni to the soup and cook for about 20 minutes, or until macaroni are tender. Pour the soup into serving bowls and top with mozzarella cheese.

9. Sausage Pasta Soup

An easy recipe, featuring Italian sausage, spinach and tomatoes.

18 oz. (500 g) **ravioli** (refrigerated)
2 oz. (55 g) **Parmesan cheese** (grated)
1 lb. (450 g) **Italian sausage** (casings removed)
3 cups **chicken stock**
3 cups **beef stock**
2 cups baby **spinach leaves** (chopped)
15 oz. (425 g) **tomatoes**
¼ cup **basil leaves** (coarsely chopped)
1 oz. **garlic**
1 oz. **oregano** (diced)

Makes 6 servings
Calories: 350 per serving

Place sausage in a large pan and cook over medium heat for 5 minutes, turning occasionally. Remove, drain and set aside.

Meanwhile, combine beef, tomatoes, chicken stock and beef stock in a large saucepan. Bring to a boil. Add ravioli and let cook for about 10 minutes. Add cooked sausage into the soup and let boil.

Stir in spinach. Once just wilted, add basil and cook for 1 more minute. Pour the soup into serving bowls, sprinkle with cheese and serve.

10. Beef Ragu with Pancetta

This dish is a perfect choice for winter. It will warm you, while rosemary adds a lovely tang to the whole dish.

14 oz. (400 g) tomatoes (diced)
2 medium carrots (halved, sliced)
2 tbs olive oil
26 oz. (750 g) gravy beef (trimmed, diced)
1 cup beef stock
1 large onion (finely chopped)
2 garlic cloves, (crushed)
2 celery stalks (sliced)
4 slices pancetta (chopped)
2 rosemary sprigs
2 tbs flour
2 bay leaves (dried)
2 tbs sage leaves (chopped)
2 thyme sprigs
2 tbs balsamic vinegar
1 cup red wine
Pasta (cooked)

Makes 4 servings
Calories: 329 per serving

Preheat oven to 350°F (180°C).

Pour half the oil in a large griddle and set over medium-high heat. Add the beef and sauté in batches for about 5 minutes each. Once the beef turns golden, transfer to a bowl.

Heat remaining oil in a skillet. Add onion, garlic, celery, carrot, and pancetta. Sauté for 5 minutes, stirring constantly. As soon as the onion is tender, stir in the beef. Add flour and let stir-cook for 1 more minute.

Add thyme, bay leaves, rosemary, sage, wine, vinegar, stock and tomato. Cover on and bring to a boil. Once boiling, transfer the griddle to the oven. Bake for 2 hours, or until beef is well cooked through. Serve with pasta.

Printed in Great Britain
by Amazon

34415777R00036